OUR LOVE STORY JOURNAL

138 QUESTIONS AND PROMPTS FOR COUPLES TO COMPLETE TOGETHER

Our Love Story Journal: 138 Questions and Prompts for Couples to Complete Together

Created by Ashley and Marcus Kusi.

ISBN-13: 978-1-949781-04-5

This love story journal belongs to

.... and ....

Our love story began on

....

Getting Started

"Life is one big love story with hundreds of little love stories within it."

-Ram Charan

Your love story is unique. One of the best ways to capture it so you don't forget it is by writing it out in a journal.

That's why we created Our Love Story Journal, a journal to help you and your partner record your love story together. This way, you can use it to reminisce memories you have shared together throughout the years from dating through marriage, or even to share your love story with friends, family, and future generations.

First, you will find 138 love story prompts and questions with spaces to help you journal your love story together. Feel free to write answers to the prompts and questions that are applicable to your love story.

Second, the love story prompts are grouped into three parts: Dating, Engagement & Wedding, and Marriage with a Love Story Index to easily find each part.

Third, at the end of each part of this love story journal, there is a space for you to paste a photo or two to help you reminisce your love story.

Lastly, complete this love story journal with your partner, because it is sure to be more fun remembering with each other as you fill it out together.

Now, get a pen and start writing your love story today!

"Being deeply loved by someone gives you strength,
while loving someone deeply gives you courage."

—Lao-Tzu

Our Love Story Index

Dating

"The best love is the kind that awakens the soul; that makes us reach for more, that plants the fire in our hearts and brings peace to our minds. That's what I hope to give you forever."

—Nicholas Sparks, The Notebook

What was life like before meeting each other?

You: ____

____

____

____

____

____

____

Me: ____

____

____

____

____

____

____

We would never have met each other if this one thing hadn't happened...

You: ____

____

____

____

____

____

____

Me: ____

____

____

____

____

____

____

The first time I saw you, I thought and felt...

You: ____

____

____

____

____

____

____

Me: ____

____

____

____

____

____

____

We were ____ and ____ years old when we met.

This is how it happened...

You: ____

____

____

____

____

____

____

Me: ____

____

____

____

____

____

____

Who pursued whom in the beginning and how?

My first impression of you was...

You: ____________________

____

____

____

____

____

____

Me: ____________________

____

____

____

____

____

____

I knew I wanted to date you after...

You: ____

____

____

____

____

____

____

Me: ____

____

____

____

____

____

____

Our first date was on ________________________________

The most memorable part of that date was...

You: ____

____

____

____

____

____

____

Me: ____

____

____

____

____

____

____

Where we had our first kiss...

How it made you feel, and what you were thinking...

You:

Me:

When we first started seeing each other, I tried to impress you by...

You: ______________________________

____

____

____

____

____

____

Me: ______________________________

____

____

____

____

____

____

We spent most of our dating period doing...

How I met your friends and what they thought of me...

You: ____

____

____

____

____

____

____

Me: ____

____

____

____

____

____

____

The first time we really laughed out loud together was...

You: ____

____

____

____

____

____

____

Me: ____

____

____

____

____

____

____

When we first met, I always described you to my friends and family as...

You: ____

____

____

____

____

____

____

Me: ____

____

____

____

____

____

____

Our favorite song or movie

Memorable movies, events, concerts, or parties we attended were...

One event that taught us so much about each other was...

You: ______________________________

____

____

____

____

____

____

Me: ______________________________

____

____

____

____

____

____

The best advice we received after we started dating...

You: ____

____

____

____

____

____

____

Me: ____

____

____

____

____

____

____

As I got to know you, what really made me fall in love with you was...

You: ____

____

____

____

____

____

____

Me: ____

____

____

____

____

____

____

The first time I knew I loved you was...
(describe the feeling)

You: ____

____

____

____

____

____

____

Me: ____

____

____

____

____

____

____

The first time I told you I loved you was...

You: ____

____

____

____

____

____

____

Me: ____

____

____

____

____

____

____

One thing that made it difficult for us to be together was...

You: ___

Me: ___

A special moment we shared while dating was...

You: ____

____

____

____

____

____

____

Me: ____

____

____

____

____

____

____

Our families' reactions and comments about the news of our relationship...

You: ____

____

____

____

____

____

____

Me: ____

____

____

____

____

____

____

When I met your family for the first time...

You: ____

____

____

____

____

____

____

Me: ____

____

____

____

____

____

____

Our families were similar and different in these ways...

Similar: ______________________________

____

____

____

____

____

____

Different: ______________________________

____

____

____

____

____

____

These people encouraged our relationship...

You: ____

____

____

____

____

____

____

Me: ____

____

____

____

____

____

____

This is how I felt most loved by you while we were dating...

You: ____

____

____

____

____

____

____

Me: ____

____

____

____

____

____

____

We shared this vision for our future...

We had to work through these differences and I had to adjust myself in these ways so we could stay together...

You: ____

____

____

____

____

____

____

Me: ____

____

____

____

____

____

____

Our relationship developed into something more serious when...

You: ____

____

____

____

____

____

____

Me: ____

____

____

____

____

____

____

Our first fight was about...

___

We resolved it by...

You: ___

___

___

___

___

___

___

Me: ___

___

___

___

___

___

___

Nicknames we called each other and the story behind them...

You: ____

____

____

____

____

____

____

Me: ____

____

____

____

____

____

____

I was scared about developing a deeper relationship with you because...

You: ____

____

____

____

____

____

____

Me: ____

____

____

____

____

____

____

Living together taught us...

You: ____

____

____

____

____

____

____

Me: ____

____

____

____

____

____

____

The best conversation we had before marriage was...

You: ____

____

____

____

____

____

____

Me: ____

____

____

____

____

____

____

How we celebrated our holidays in the beginning of our relationship...

Our favorite ways to relax together while dating were...

You: ____

____

____

____

____

____

____

Me: ____

____

____

____

____

____

____

Other great memories of our dating period...

Other great memories of our dating period...

Our favorite photos from when we were dating

Engagement & Wedding

"Love is composed of a single soul inhabiting two bodies."

–Aristotle

I knew you were the one when...

You: ____

____

____

____

____

____

____

Me: ____

____

____

____

____

____

____

What qualities did I have that made you want to spend your life with me?

You: ______________________________

____

____

____

____

____

____

Me: ______________________________

____

____

____

____

____

____

What happened the day you asked your partner to marry you? How did you feel?

You: ____

____

____

____

____

____

What happened when your partner asked you to marry them? How did you feel?

Me: ____

____

____

____

____

____

I spoke to the following people about marrying you before I proposed/accepted, and their advice was...

You: ____

____

____

____

____

____

____

Me: ____

____

____

____

____

____

____

This is how we announced our engagement...

Some of the most memorable reactions to our engagement were...

Our families' reactions and comments about the news of our engagement...

You: ____

____

____

____

____

____

____

Me: ____

____

____

____

____

____

____

Where we picked out our engagement and wedding rings and why we chose them...

Why we chose to change or not change one of our last names...

Where we spent the night before the wedding...

Memorable mentions from our pre-wedding parties...

Funny things that happened the day of our wedding...

Who was in our wedding and why we chose them...

The wedding location and what made it so special...

This is what I felt and what I was thinking right before the big moment...

You: ____

____

____

____

____

____

____

Me: ____

____

____

____

____

____

____

Memorable conversations before the ceremony...

You: ___

Me: ___

Moments getting ready for the ceremony were spent...

You: ______________________________

____

____

____

____

____

____

Me: ______________________________

____

____

____

____

____

____

Most memorable moments of our wedding ceremony...

You: ____

____

____

____

____

____

____

Me: ____

____

____

____

____

____

____

Our marriage vows meant...

You: ____

____

____

____

____

____

____

Me: ____

____

____

____

____

____

____

Most memorable moments of our wedding reception...

My favorite part of our wedding day was...

You: ____

____

____

____

____

____

____

Me: ____

____

____

____

____

____

____

What I remember most about our wedding night was...

You: ___

Me: ___

This is how we celebrated our honeymoon...

Most memorable moments of our honeymoon...

You: ____________________

Me: ____________________

What we looked forward to most about spending the rest of our lives together...

You: ____

____

____

____

____

____

____

Me: ____

____

____

____

____

____

____

The future marriage we dreamed of having when we first got engaged...

You: ______________________________

____

____

____

____

____

____

Me: ______________________________

____

____

____

____

____

____

Other great memories from this period in our lives...

Other great memories from this period in our lives...

Our favorite engagement pictures

Our favorite wedding pictures

Marriage

"Love is a choice you make from moment to moment."

–Barbara De Angelis

The first place we lived after we got married and what we remember most about it was...

You: ____

____

____

____

____

____

____

Me: ____

____

____

____

____

____

____

In the beginning of our marriage, this is how we handled the finances, what made it difficult, and how we worked it out...

A goal or life dream that we shared in the beginning of our marriage was...

Couples who inspired us, who we looked up to, and why...

When it came to growing our family, we originally decided...

If we got pregnant, when we found out, we felt and reacted...

You: ____

____

____

____

____

____

____

Me: ____

____

____

____

____

____

____

If we had children, the most memorable moments of the pregnancy and birth experience(s) were...

You: ______________________________

____

____

____

____

____

____

Me: ______________________________

____

____

____

____

____

____

If we had children, they changed our relationship in these ways...

The hardest thing about parenting was...

You: ____

____

____

____

____

____

____

Me: ____

____

____

____

____

____

____

The best thing about being parents...

You: ____

____

____

____

____

____

____

Me: ____

____

____

____

____

____

____

Biggest lesson we learned from our first year of marriage...

You: ______________________________

____

____

____

____

____

____

Me: ______________________________

____

____

____

____

____

____

Special moments we shared together in the time we have been together (happy, sad, moving or profound)...

How the vision we shared for our future changed throughout the years...

The most exciting place we have been intimate outside our bedroom was...

The riskiest place we were ever intimate was...

What qualities make our relationship strong and unique...

We had to work through these differences and adjust ourselves in these ways to have a healthy marriage...

Five things I appreciate most about you are...

You:

1. ______________________________

2. ______________________________

3. ______________________________

4. ______________________________

5. ______________________________

Me:

1. ______________________________

2. ______________________________

3. ______________________________

4. ______________________________

5. ______________________________

Some of the most romantic moments throughout the time we have been together are...

You: ____

____

____

____

____

____

____

Me: ____

____

____

____

____

____

____

Memorable trips we have taken...

Our most memorable wedding anniversary celebration was...

You: ____________________

Me: ____________________

These differences in our personalities made us stronger as a couple...

Unspoken expectations we had pertaining to marriage...

You: ____

____

____

____

____

____

____

Me: ____

____

____

____

____

____

____

The longest time we were apart and how we got through it...

Moments when we had to reevaluate our marriage or I was afraid I might lose you for good...

I was the proudest to be your partner in life when...

You: ______________________________

____

____

____

____

____

____

Me: ______________________________

____

____

____

____

____

____

How celebrating holidays has changed over the years for us...

The holiday traditions we started together...

These events in the world affected us...

Our favorite birthday celebrations since we have been married are...

You: ____

____

____

____

____

____

____

Me: ____

____

____

____

____

____

____

One thing we have loved creating/ building together has been...

How I felt the most supported by you throughout our marriage...

You: ____

____

____

____

____

____

____

Me: ____

____

____

____

____

____

____

New adventures we experienced together over the years...

The most difficult financial times for us, how we got through them, and what we learned...

Things that challenged our marriage...

What we have learned from each other over the time we have been married...

You: ____

____

____

____

____

____

____

Me: ____

____

____

____

____

____

____

People we spent a lot of time with and the fun things we did with them...

This is how our relationship has evolved over the years...

A goal or life dream that we share now...

The biggest crisis we have experienced together and how we came out stronger...

Some of the hardest health issues we have experienced and how we overcame them together...

The sweetest thing we have done for each other...

You: ___

Me: ___

Craziest or scariest things we have done together...

Things we have accomplished because of each other...

Our most memorable disagreements and how we resolved them...

This is how we learned to disagree with each other...

Our most embarrassing moment as a couple...

Our most embarrassing moment as parents...

If you had not been in my life, I never would have...

You: ____

____

____

____

____

____

____

Me: ____

____

____

____

____

____

____

What I love most about you...

You: ____________________

Me: ____________________

How our love has grown and changed over time...

You: ____

____

____

____

____

____

____

Me: ____

____

____

____

____

____

____

How I would describe you to a third person...

You: ______________________________

____

____

____

____

____

____

Me: ______________________________

____

____

____

____

____

____

What is at least one small gesture that I do for you regularly, that you appreciate?

You: ____

____

____

____

____

____

____

Me: ____

____

____

____

____

____

____

Things we do to keep romance alive in our relationship...

How we have been intentional about growing together as a couple...

How would you summarize the years we have been together in one word?

You: ____

Me: ____

How we remained independent and interdependent in our relationship...

You: ____

____

____

____

____

Me: ____

____

____

____

____

How has your world view changed since we met?

You: ____

____

____

____

____

____

____

Me: ____

____

____

____

____

____

____

Things we have accomplished together as a couple...

Books that have made an impact on our life and relationship are...

Lessons about marriage we want to share with you are...

What I look forward to most about the years ahead of us...

You: ____

____

____

____

____

____

____

Me: ____

____

____

____

____

____

____

My favorite thing about our love story is...

You: ____

Me: ____

Other special moments we want to remember throughout our marriage.

Other special moments we want to remember throughout our marriage.

Some of our favorite photos from throughout the years

Some of our favorite photos from throughout the years

Some of our favorite photos from throughout the years

Some of our favorite photos from throughout the years

We completed this journal on

....

Thank You

Thank you for choosing *Our Love Story Journal* to record your love story together.

If you enjoyed using this book, please leave a review on Amazon and share the book with other couples. You can even gift this book as an engagement, wedding, or anniversary gift to your friends and family.

If you would like to receive email updates about future books, courses, and more, visit our website today to join our book fan community:

www.ourpeacefulfamily.com/bookfan

Thank you again for choosing our journal!

Ashley and Marcus Kusi

About the Authors

Marcus and Ashley help overwhelmed newlyweds adjust to married life and inspire married couples to improve their marriage so they can become better husbands and wives.

They do this by using their own marriage experience, gleaning wisdom from other married couples, and sharing what works for them through their website and marriage podcast, *The First Year Marriage Show.*

Visit the following website to listen to their podcast:

www.firstyearmarriage.com

To learn more about them, visit *www.ourpeacefulfamily.com*

"Marriage is a lifelong journey that thrives on love, commitment, trust, respect, communication, patience, and companionship."

–Ashley and Marcus Kusi

Other Books by Ashley and Marcus

1. Our Bucket List Adventures: A Journal for Couples
2. Our Gratitude Journal: 52 Weeks of Love, Mindfulness, and Appreciation for Couples
3. Questions for Couples: 469 Thought-Provoking Conversation Starters for Connecting, Building Trust, and Rekindling Intimacy
4. Communication in Marriage: How to Communicate with Your Spouse Without Fighting
5. First Year of Marriage: The Newlywed's Guide to Building a Strong Foundation and Adjusting to Married Life.
6. Emotional and Sexual Intimacy in Marriage: How to Connect or Reconnect with Your Spouse, Grow Together, and Strengthen Your Marriage